Clemmie

Walter Clement Noel
and the Discovery of
Sickle Cell Disease

Written by Chanel Arrington • Illustrated by DG

Published by InspiHeard Now, LLC
Budd Lake, New Jersey
Library of Congress Control Number: 2021908114
Copyright © 2021 by InspiHeard Now, LLC

ISBN: 978-0-578-88593-3

Editing, Illustrations, Book Cover Design, Layout, & Formatting by DG Self-Publishing
www.dgselfpublishing.com

DEDiCATiON

This book is dedicated to all, past, present, and future, living with sickle cell disease and to those who care for them; to my shining star, Carsyn, who always sparkles; to Caitlyn, with her heart of gold; to my love, Craig; and to all of my family and friends who love, support, and encourage me in my journey.

ACKNOWLEDGMENTS

I am forever grateful to God and acknowledge Him in all that I do.

"Trust in the Lord with all your heart, and do not lean on your own understanding. In all your ways acknowledge Him, and He will make straight your paths" (Proverbs 3:5–6 ESV).

This book would not have been possible without the contributions of Todd Savitt, PhD. Dr. Savitt, through your years of research, we know his name—Walter Clement "Clemmie" Noel. Your research in African American medical history is significant beyond measure. I am grateful for my years of working with you at Brody School of Medicine at East Carolina University. Your dedication to advocating for and teaching about diversity in medicine is valuable to all. Thank you for entrusting me with the gift of sharing your research with future generations. The sickle cell community is fortunate to have you as an educator and advocate.

On the colorful, sun-soaked Caribbean Island of Grenada, Walter Clement Noel grew up on the land owned by his mother.

Duquesne (pronounced "Doo-kane") Estate was Clemmie's playground. It was surrounded by tree- and brush-covered mountains and farmland that grew fruits, vegetables, and spices. The warm turquoise-blue waters of the Caribbean Sea sparkled in the distance.

Like his brother and sisters, Clemmie spent his childhood running barefoot through the brush and the streets of the nearby town, starting his collection of bruises, sores, and scratches. But there was something inside Clemmie that made him a little different.

He had a mysterious sickness that would show up throughout his life. His own personal villain that did not yet have a name. Clemmie's mom, dad, brother, and sisters did not have this same sickness, so they did not know just how awful it made him feel at times.

This mysterious villain was later named sickle cell disease.

Peeking its crescent moon-shaped head whenever *it* felt like it, the sickness brought pains, fevers, and aches that became a part of Clemmie's life.

So, have you ever heard of sickle cell disease? Let's talk about it. It's a blood disorder that millions of people in the world have.

It's something people are born with because of genes they get from their parents.

People in certain parts of the world are more likely than others to have sickle cell or the genes that cause sickle cell disease.

Did you know that in people with sickle cell disease, some of the red blood cells that are usually round like a donut become hard, sticky, and shaped like a crescent moon or sickle? When this happens, the sickled red blood cells do not flow easily through the blood vessels of the body.

Even though this sickness can cause a lot of pain and scary health problems, adults, teens, and kids living with sickle cell disease still try to live great lives like everyone else. People living with sickle cell disease can have big dreams, too, and want to make a difference in the world. They are undercover warriors who have amazing superpowers! (Well, maybe that last part is only a little bit true!)

When Clemmie was growing up, no one knew about sickle cell disease. Clemmie and his family just knew that he got very sick at times and had a few sores on his ankles, legs, and arms. Sometimes his heart beat too fast, and he had trouble breathing. Clemmie also had some of the same sicknesses that other kids had, such as the infection with a funny-sounding name called yaws, which left him with more sores on his legs. Clemmie couldn't catch a break!

Still, he didn't let his sicknesses or anything else hold him back. He had big dreams!

When Clemmie was a teenager, he dreamed of becoming a dentist like his friend Oliver Charles Arthur. Oliver was only five years older than Clemmie and went far away to a college in America to become a dentist. When he returned to Grenada, Oliver opened two dental offices to serve his people. Dr. Arthur was the only licensed dentist on the whole island!

Clemmie was inspired!

Little did he know that something even greater, something that would impact the world forever, was going to happen because he would be in the right place at the **most** perfect time.

As Clemmie prepared for college, Dr. Arthur helped him by writing letters to two faraway dental schools. Clemmie decided that the school for him was in Chicago, Illinois, in the United States, over 2,500 miles from his sun-soaked island of Grenada.

Clemmie's mother also supported his dream and wanted to make sure her son would be okay so far from home. She even wrote a letter to the person in charge of the college!

Now twenty years old, Clemmie began a new adventure. He boarded a ship from the nearby island of Barbados, starting his eight-day sea journey to the port of New York City with $70 in his pocket.

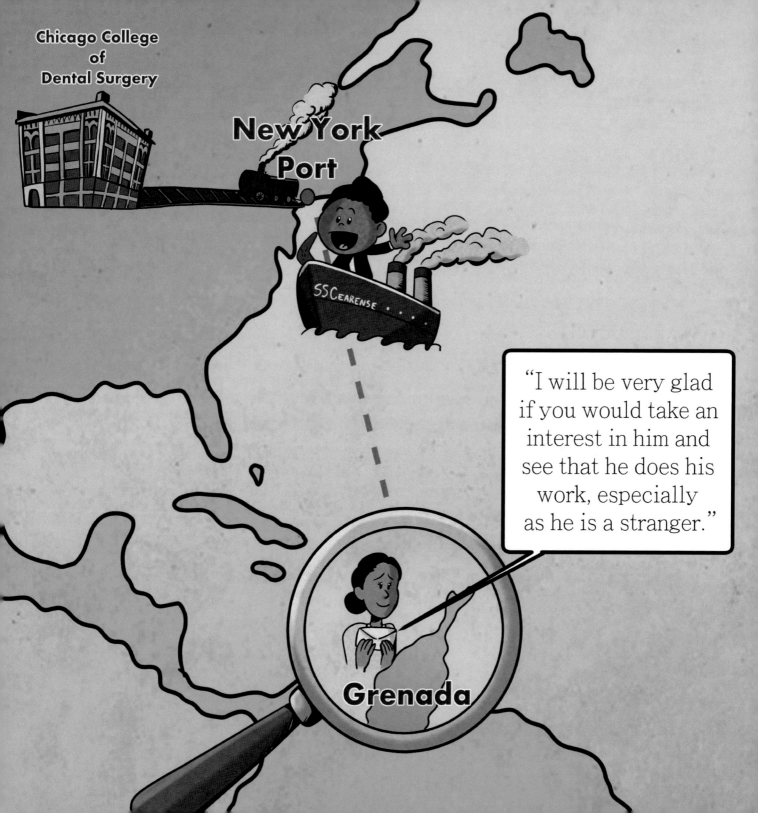

Clemmie was very adventurous, but there was a villain lurking—that crescent moon-shaped sickness that still showed up at random times in Clemmie's body. Remember? While on the ship to New York, it showed up again, this time in the form of a painful sore on his ankle called an ulcer. The ulcer healed in about a week but left a scar that added to the scars and scratches he already had on his arms and legs. Clemmie didn't know that this kind of ulcer can be common in people living with sickle cell disease.

Even with the challenge of the ulcer, Clemmie warriored on and didn't let it stop him. Off to Chicago from New York.

Finally, Clemmie arrived in Chicago and settled into his rented room close to the college. On an October evening before classes started, Clemmie met his teachers and the other students . . . and he noticed something.

This was a lot different from his sun-soaked island of Grenada. Even though he was a stranger in a strange land, Clemmie didn't let this challenge get in his way of being another step closer to becoming a dentist.

Around Thanksgiving, only a few months after starting college, Clemmie got sick. His sickness lasted all the way to Christmas. That's about five weeks!

On the day after Christmas, Clemmie found his way to the hospital near his college. There, he was examined by Dr. Ernest Irons, who saw, under a microscope, something in Clemmie's blood that no one had ever seen before. Those crescent moon-shaped blood cells! Clemmie's red blood cells were so mysterious that Dr. Irons had to ask another doctor, James Herrick, to take a look. They were both puzzled.

Clemmie felt awful. He stayed in the hospital for a month. Doctors looked closely at him—poking, sticking, testing. But Clemmie's crescent-shaped blood cells did not fit the description of any of the sicknesses known at that time. So, the mystery continued. In the meantime, Clemmie had to go back to college.

Over the next few years of school, Clemmie's sickness appeared at least four more times. And just before he finished dental school, it happened again.

This time, Clemmie stayed in the hospital for two long months, fighting the mysterious sickness. He won this fight just in time to finish school. All along, Clemmie was determined to keep up with his schoolwork. Now it was finally time for graduation!

Even with the many challenges he faced, Clemmie still graduated with his classmates. He finally achieved his dream of becoming a dentist! Clemmie never gave up.

But the story isn't over just yet.

Back home in the busy town of St. George's, Grenada, Clemmie opened his dental office in a building his mother owned. He lived there, too, in an apartment above the office. Even though his crescent moon-shaped villain still lurked about, he didn't let that stop him from living happily in his sun-soaked home country, being a dentist and spending time with his family and friends.

Unknown to Clemmie, Dr. Herrick, one of the curious doctors who had cared for him in Chicago, wrote an article describing his never-before-seen condition. This led to it being known to the world. A few years later, after Clemmie's lifetime, the sickness was named sickle cell disease because of the crescent moon– or "sickle"-shaped blood cells described by that doctor. The lifelong villain that challenged Clemmie in the scariest ways finally had a name!

Peculiar Elongated
and
Sickle-Shaped
Red Blood Corpuscles
in a Case of Severe Anemia

James B. Herrick, M.D., Chicago

Clemmie was the VERY FIRST person known to have sickle cell disease! Even though the disease surely existed long before Clemmie's life, it was because of his being in the right place at the most perfect time that the discovery happened. Because of Clemmie's dream of doing something big—his dream of going to college in a place over 2,500 miles from his island of Grenada . . . his dream of becoming a dentist . . . and his dream of making a difference to the people of his country—Clemmie was able to make an impact on the medical world and on other people living with sickle cell disease . . . an impact beyond his wildest dreams.

[Mary Justina Noel (mother)]

CLEMMIE'S LIFE TIMELINE

June 21, 1884

born to Mary Justina Noel and John Cornelius Noel, St. Patrick's Parish, Grenada

February 1886

father, John Cornelius Noel, died at age 36

Mid-1890s–1901

attended high school in St. George's, Grenada, and Harrison's College in Bridgetown, Barbados

September 1904

traveled by ship from Bridgetown, Barbados, to New York City, then by train to Chicago

October 5, 1904

began studies at Chicago College of Dental Surgery

December 26, 1904

went to Presbyterian Hospital for medical care for respiratory illness—admitted and treated by Dr. Ernest Irons. Irons noted many crescent-shaped, elongated red blood cells in Noel's microscopic blood exam and mentioned this unusual finding to his mentor, Dr. James Herrick

[Building that housed Noel's office, 1907-1916, St. George's, Grenada, 2010]

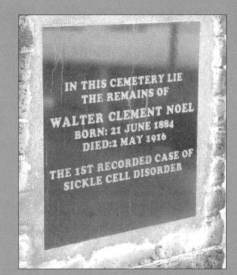

[Plaque at Cemetery, Sauteurs, Grenada, 2010]

1905–1907

continued his studies in dental school, but got sick many times. Treated by Drs. Irons and Herrick, always displaying in his blood examination the sickle-shaped blood cells and anemia symptoms

May 28, 1907

graduated from Chicago College of Dental Surgery and returned to Grenada

1907–1916

lived in St. George's and practiced dentistry, one of only a few dentists in Grenada

1910

Dr. Herrick published WCN's case in a medical journal (the first published and documented case of what became known as sickle cell anemia, now called sickle cell disease)

May 3, 1916

died of pneumonia. Was never in touch with his former physicians in Chicago and never read the medical journal article about his case

1922

a fourth case similar to WCN's was recognized and described in a medical journal. The author, Dr. Verne Mason of Los Angeles, named the disorder "sickle cell anemia"

1923 and beyond

many physicians began to recognize, study, and learn how to treat sickle cell anemia in their patients. Today, the disease is recognized globally

SOURCES

"Herrick's 1910 Case Report of Sickle Cell Anemia: The Rest of the Story" by Todd L. Savitt, Morton F. Goldberg (*JAMA*. Volume 261, 1989, pp. 266-271)

"Peculiar Elongated and Sickle-Shaped Red Blood Corpuscles in a Case of Severe Anemia" by James B. Herrick (*Archives of Internal Medicine*. Volume 6, 1910, pp. 517-521)

"Tracking Down the First Recorded Sickle Cell Patient in Western Medicine" by Todd L. Savitt (*Journal of the National Medical Association*. Volume 102, 2010, pp. 981-992)

SICKLE CELL RESOURCES

Sickle Cell Disease Association of America (SCDAA)
https://www.sicklecelldisease.org

Centers for Disease Control and Prevention (CDC)
https://www.cdc.gov/ncbddd/sicklecell/index.html

National Heart, Lung, and Blood Institute (NIH NHLBI)
https://www.nhlbi.nih.gov/health-topics/sickle-cell-disease

ABOUT THE AUTHOR

Chanel Arrington is passionate about using her creativity for projects that inspire and educate. She is a wife, mom, entrepreneur, and advocate. Chanel graduated from the University of North Carolina at Chapel Hill with a Bachelor of Arts in Communication Studies. Chanel and her family are on a continuous journey, learning about sickle cell disease while advocating for her youngest daughter, Carsyn. Carsyn's spirit of courage and perseverance is the inspiration for Chanel's work educating others about sickle cell disease.

SHARE YOUR FEEDBACK!

Did you enjoy this book? Please post a review on Amazon to let others know about your experience. Your review will help with getting this book into the hands of more children, and we would love to hear your feedback!

Sickle cell disease is always there, even when the person living with the condition feels well and may not be experiencing pain or symptoms. How many pictures of the crescent-shaped cell can you find throughout the story?

Made in United States
Orlando, FL
10 December 2021